P9-CRW-404

WHAT'S THE
WEATHER?

Shelley Rotner

HOLIDAY HOUSE • NEW YORK

What's the weather outside?

Is it hot or cold?

Sunny, cloudy, rainy, snowy, or windy?

Weather affects all living things.

Depending on where you live,
weather is always changing,
day to day and season to season.

Winter
is cold.
Sometimes
it snows.
We bundle up.

Spring
is warm.
Flowers
bloom.
We grow
gardens.

Summer
is hot.
Fruits are ripe.
We splash
and swim.

Autumn
is cool.
Leaves
turn colors.
We pick
pumpkins.

11

Some places, like deserts, are hot and dry all day long.

Other places, like the North and South Poles, are always cold.

Rainforests
are always wet.
It rains almost every day
all year round.

Wind can change weather by moving air.

Air is all around you— at your house, on the playground, and even in you!

You can't see air. You only know it's there
because it makes things move. Some days feel
colder because of the wind. This is called wind chill.

Wind moves clouds too, from one place to another.

Different kinds of clouds bring different kinds of weather.

Do the shapes of clouds
remind you of anything?

Fog is a kind of cloud that forms close
to the ground. When you walk through fog,
you are actually walking through a cloud!

Have you ever gone to the beach
on a sunny day and all of a sudden
the fog rolls in?

It rains
when clouds
get heavy
and fill with
drops of water
that fall.

Rainstorms can produce thunder and lightning.

Sometimes we can see a rainbow
when part of the sky is cloudy and rainy
and part of the sky is sunny.

The sunlight shines
through the raindrops
and makes an arc of colors
called a rainbow.

It snows when the temperature
is low and clouds get heavy
and fill with drops of water
that freeze and fall to the ground.
Blizzards are snowstorms
with strong winds and
lots of snowfall.

Weather can be extreme.

Hurricanes are intense tropical rainstorms with strong winds. The storm clouds swirl.

Hurricanes can cause flooding and power outages.

HIGH WATER

Sometimes rain can freeze. When rain freezes before it makes contact with the ground, it's called sleet. When small lumps of ice and snow fall from clouds, it's called hail.

Tornados are even stronger storms called twisters. The air spins like a top and picks up dirt, tree branches, and anything in its way—even houses.

Meteorologists
try to predict
the weather
so we can plan
and be prepared.

Climatologists
help by looking at
weather patterns
over time
to learn
how our climate
is changing.
The weather
is becoming
more unpredictable.

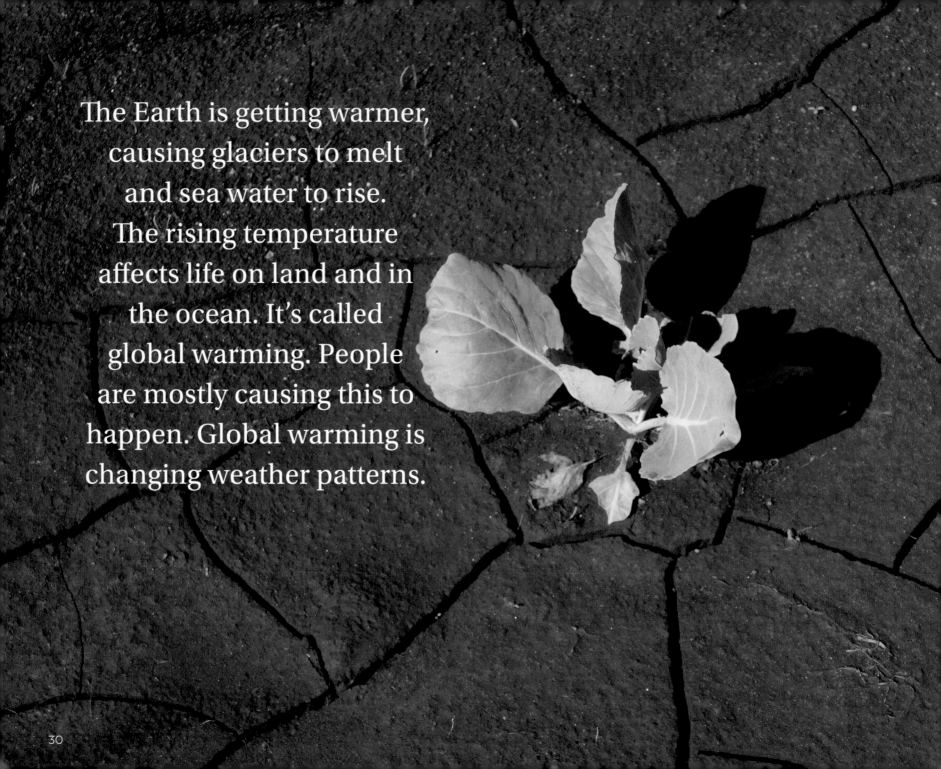

The Earth is getting warmer,
causing glaciers to melt
and sea water to rise.
The rising temperature
affects life on land and in
the ocean. It's called
global warming. People
are mostly causing this to
happen. Global warming is
changing weather patterns.

These changes are called climate change. Now, there are more times with lots of rain and flooding and more times without any rain, called droughts. There are more extreme storms, heat waves, cold spells, and frequent wildfires. These changes are causing problems for plants and trees, for animals, and for people too.

Protect The Earth...
Ride, Don't Drive.

There are many different ways people can help
slow down climate change by taking
better care of our Earth.

If we work together, we can help everyone have
clean air and water and healthy food.

Glossary

Blizzard: a long-lasting snowstorm with very strong winds and lots of snowfall

Climate: the pattern of weather in an area over a long period of time

Climate change: a change in the usual weather found in a place

Climatologist: a scientist who studies climate and climate change

Cloud: a mass of tiny water droplets in the sky

Desert: a dry region that gets very little rain

Drought: a period when it doesn't rain for a long time and everything becomes dry

Fog: a cloud of water droplets that forms near the ground

Global warming: the rising of temperatures on Earth

Hail: small lumps of ice and snow that fall from the clouds sometimes during thunderstorms

Hurricane: a severe storm with spiraling winds

Lightning: an electrical charge that travels between a cloud and the ground

Meteorologist: a scientist who tries to predict what the weather will be

North and South Poles: the southernmost and northernmost surfaces on Earth

Rainbow: an arc of colors that appears in the sky opposite the sun, caused by the sun shining through rain or mist

Rain forest: a forest with tall trees, warm climates, and daily rain

Sleet: a mixture of snow and rain as well as raindrops that freeze on their way down

Temperature: a measurement of hotness or coldness

Thunder: a loud, booming noise that follows lightning during a storm

Tornado: a powerful whirling wind with a funnel-shaped cloud that moves over the land and often destroys things in its path

Weather: the daily wind, temperature, and atmosphere

Wind: air that moves

Wind chill: how cold the wind feels on a human body; a combination of temperature and wind speed

In memory of my mom

Copyright © 2019 by Shelley Rotner
All Rights Reserved
HOLIDAY HOUSE is registered in the U.S. Patent and Trademark Office.
Printed and bound in November 2019 at Tien Wah Press, Johor Bahru, Johor, Malaysia.
www.holidayhouse.com
First Edition
1 3 5 7 9 10 8 6 4 2

Library of Congress Cataloging-in-Publication Data
Names: Rotner, Shelley, author.
Title: What's the weather? / Shelley Rotner.
Other titles: What is the weather?
Description: First edition. | New York : Holiday House, [2020] |
Audience: Age 3-7. | Audience: K to grade 3.
Identifiers: LCCN 2019013575 | ISBN 9780823443499 (hardcover)
Subjects: LCSH: Weather—Juvenile literature.
Classification: LCC QC981.3 .R6648 2020 | DDC 551.5—dc23
LC record available at https://lccn.loc.gov/2019013575

Photo credits: iStock.com/Leonsbox, p. 13; iStock.com/Slavicia, p. 21; iStock.com/Mike Mareen,
p. 26 bottom left; iStock.com/Chknox, p. 26 bottom right; iStock.com/Clint Spencer, p. 28; iStock.com/Sepp
Frieduber, p. 31 top; iStock.com/Mile High Traveler, p. 31 bottom.

Special thanks to designer Katie Craig

The author would also like to thank meteorologist Jacob Wycoff of Western Mass News on WGGB,
an ABC affiliate, for sharing his expertise, and to climatologist Kinuyo Kanamaru, Assistant Professor
of Geosciences at the University of Massachusetts–Amherst, for her help and for vetting the text
and photographs for accuracy.

Carbon dioxide is a gas found in the air we breathe. Though we cannot see this gas, it acts like a blanket that helps keep us and our planet warm. Without carbon dioxide, we would feel much colder! Carbon dioxide allows us and all other living organisms on our planet to live comfortably.

Recently, the amount of carbon dioxide added into our air has increased faster than we have ever seen in our Earth's history, causing climate change. This is because most of the carbon dioxide in our air today comes from fossil fuels that we burn to power our factories, homes, trains, cars, buses, and airplanes. As we burn more fossil fuel, we add more carbon dioxide into our air. With increasing amounts of carbon dioxide, our Earth becomes warmer and warmer! For this reason, it is very important that we carefully manage the amount of fossil fuel we burn so that we and our Earth do not become too hot!

—Kinuyo Kanamaru, *climatologist*